EASY GUITAR
WITH NOTES & TAB

The Best of
The Allman Brothers

T0058960

2 **Strum and Pick Patterns**

3 **Ain't Wastin' Time No More**

8 **Black Hearted Woman**

11 **Blue Sky**

14 **Come and Go Blues**

18 **End of the Line**

22 **Good Clean Fun**

26 **It's Not My Cross to Bear**

29 **Melissa**

32 **Midnight Rider**

33 **Pony Boy**

36 **Ramblin' Man**

39 **Seven Turns**

42 **Southbound**

44 **Stand Back**

47 **Statesboro Blues**

52 **Straight from the Heart**

58 **Trouble No More**

55 **Wasted Words**

62 **Whipping Post**

ISBN 978-0-7935-7359-2

HAL•LEONARD®
CORPORATION

7777 W. BLUEMOUND RD. P.O. BOX 13819 MILWAUKEE, WI 53213

Visit Hal Leonard Online at
www.halleonard.com

STRUM AND PICK PATTERNS

This chart contains the suggested strum and pick patterns that are referred to by number at the beginning of each song in this book. The symbols ⊓ and ∨ in the strum patterns refer to down and up strokes, respectively. The letters in the pick patterns indicate which right-hand fingers plays which strings.

p = **thumb**
i = **index finger**
m = **middle finger**
a = **ring finger**

For example; Pick Pattern 2
is played: thumb - index - middle - ring

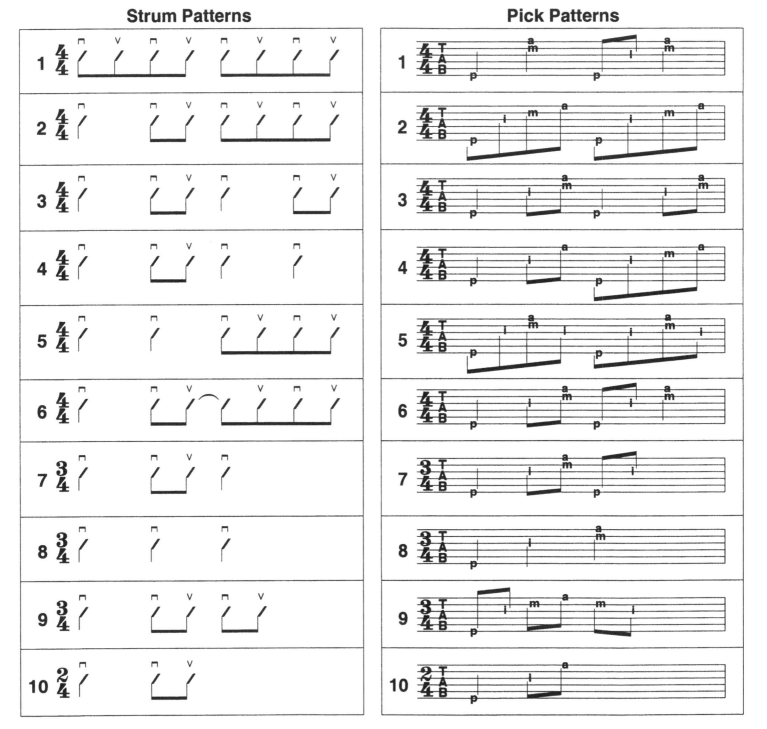

You can use the 3/4 Strum or Pick Patterns in songs written in compound meter (6/8, 9/8, 12/8, etc.).
For example, you can accompany a song in 6/8 by playing the 3/4 pattern twice in each measure.
The 4/4 Strum and Pick Patterns can be used for songs written in cut time (¢) by doubling the note time values in the patterns. Each pattern would therefore last two measures in cut time.

Ain't Wastin' Time No More

Words and Music by Gregg Allman

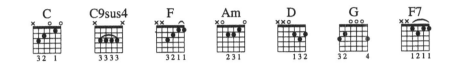

C   C9sus4   F   Am   D   G   F7

Strum Pattern: 3
Pick Pattern: 1

Intro
Fast Rock

% Verse

1. Last Sun-day morn-
3. *See Additional Lyrics*

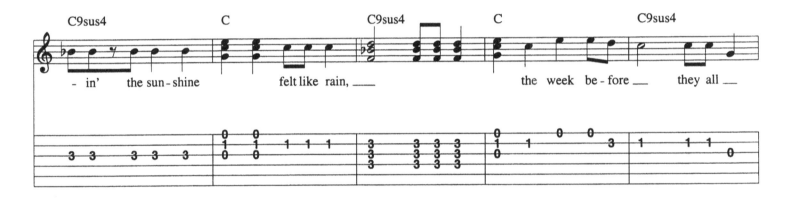

- in' the sun-shine   felt like rain, ___   the week be-fore ___   they all ___

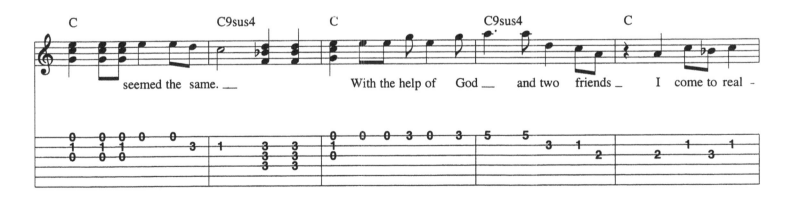

seemed the same. ___   With the help of God ___ and two friends ___ I come to real -

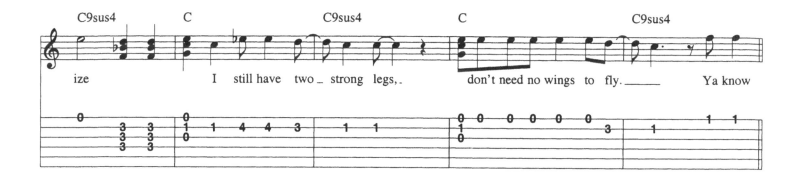

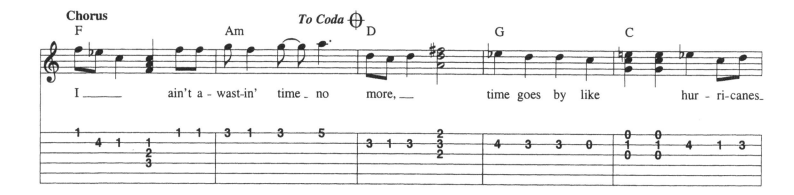

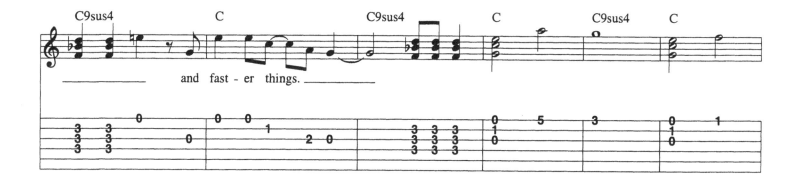

Been a-round here three long days, ___ look-in' like you're dy - in'. ___ Just step your-self

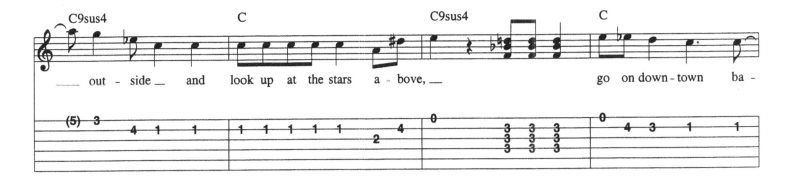

___ out - side ___ and look up at the stars a - bove, ___ go on down-town ba -

- by, find ___ some - bod - y to love. ___ A mean-while I ___ ain't a -

Chorus

wast - in' time ___ no ___ more. ___ 'Cause time goes by ___ like ___ pour - in' rain ___

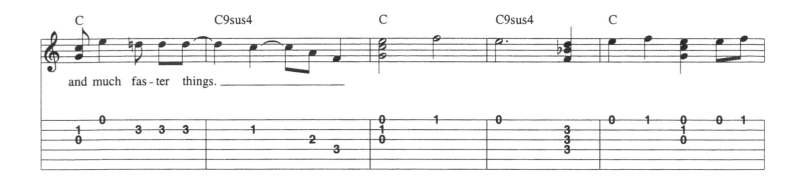

and much fas-ter things.

Bridge

You don't need _ no _ gyp-sy to tell ya why _

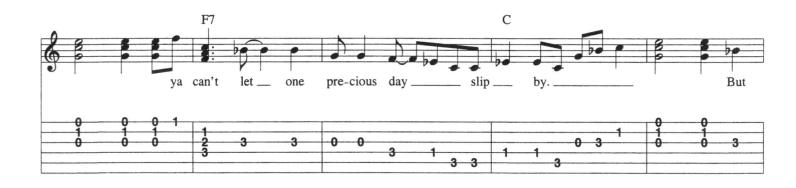

ya can't let _ one pre-cious day _ slip _ by. _ But

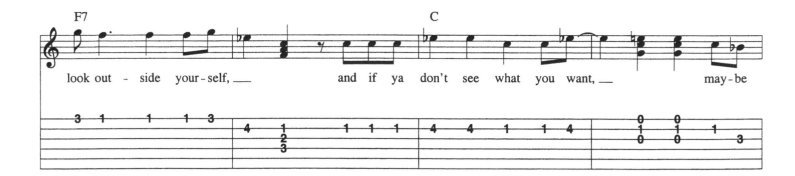

look out - side your-self, _ and if ya don't see what you want, _ may-be

some-times then you don't. ___ Well leave ___ your mind a - lone ___ and just get high. ___

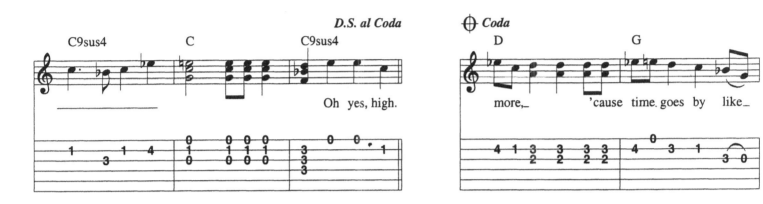

___ Oh yes, high.

more, ___ 'cause time goes by like ___

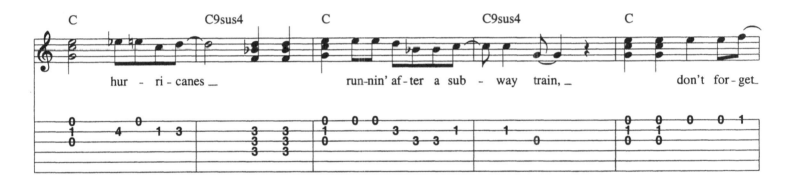

hur - ri - canes ___ run-nin' af-ter a sub - way train, ___ don't for-get ___

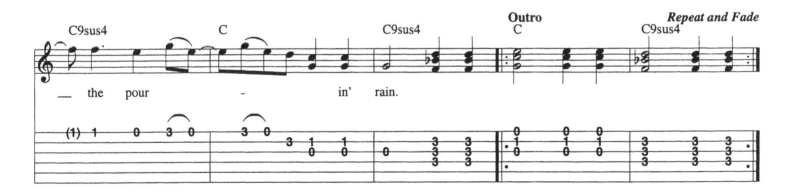

___ the pour - in' rain.

Additional Lyrics

3. I found my way after many years are gone,
   And all the war freaks die off, leavin' us alone.
   Well now children, leave in peace the way we came.
   'Cept for you and me brother, try and try again.
   So hear us now. We ain't wastin' time no more,
   Time goes by like hurricanes and faster things.

Black Hearted Woman

Words and Music by Gregg Allman

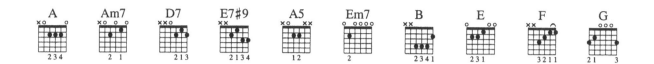

Strum Pattern: 3
Pick Pattern: 4

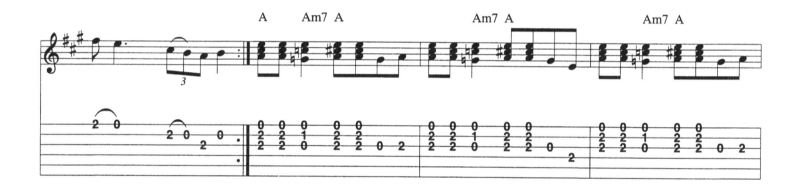

Ah, ah, ah, ah, ah, __ ah, ah. Ah, ah, ah, __ ah. Ah, ah, ah __ ah, ah, ah, ah,

ah, ah, ah, _ ah. __ Ah, ah, ah, ah, ah, __ ah, ah. Ah, ah, ah, __ ah. Ah, ah, ah, __ ah, ah, ah, ah,

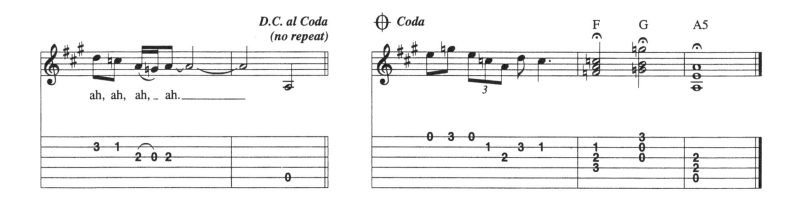

ah, ah, ah, _ ah. _____

Additional Lyrics

2. Black hearted woman, cheap trouble, and pain is all you play.
   Black hearted woman, cheap trouble, and pain is all you play.
   Sometime thinking I'll be better, if I was stiff down in my grave.
   No, I just can't stay.

3. Yesterday I was your man, now you don't know my name.
   Yesterday I was your man, now you don't know my name.
   Well I'm going out to find a new way babe, oh, to get back into your game.
   Yeah, yeah.

4. One of these days, I'm gonna catch you with your back door man,
   One of these days, yeah, I'm gonna catch you with your back door man,
   I'll be moving on down the road pretty baby, oh, to start all over again.
   Oh, yeah.

Blue Sky

Words and Music by Dickey Betts

Strum Pattern: 3, 4
Pick Pattern: 3, 5

Intro
Moderately Fast

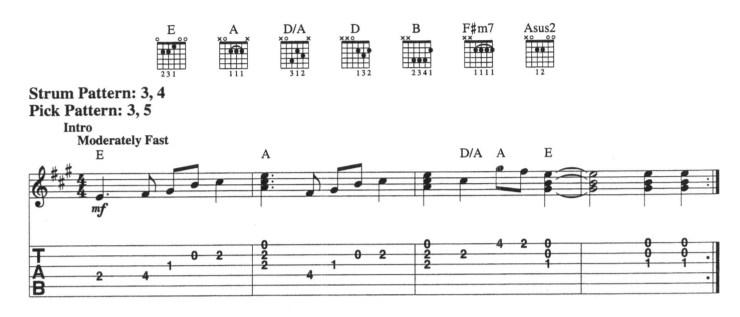

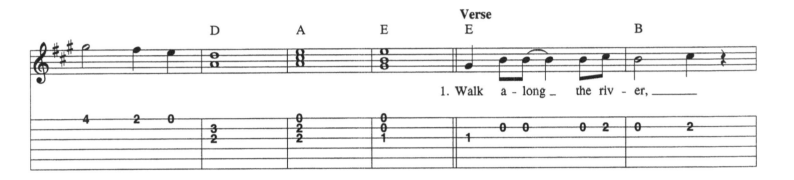

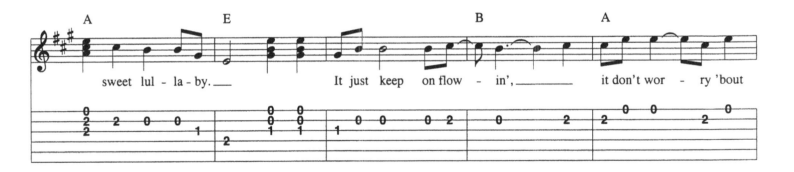

2. Don't fly Mis-ter Blue - bird, I'm just walk-in' down the road. _ Ear-ly morn - in' sun -
3. *See Additional Lyrics*

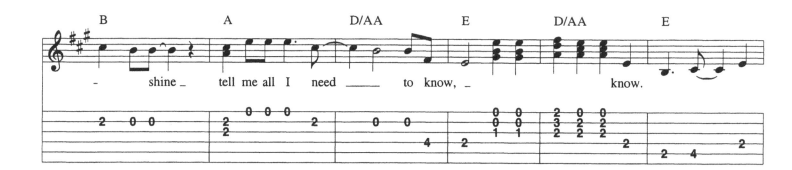

- shine _ tell me all I need _____ to know, _ know.

You're my _ blue sky, _

you're my sun - ny day. _ Lord, you know it makes _ me high _ when you turn your love _ my

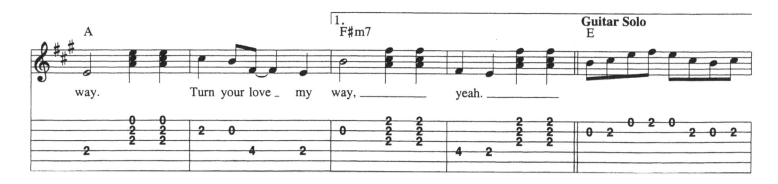

way. Turn your love _ my way, _____ yeah. _____

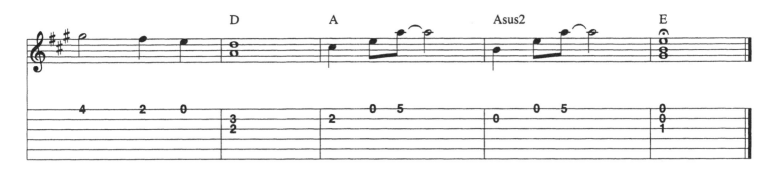

Additional Lyrics

3. Good old Sunday morning, bells are ringin' everywhere.
   Goin' to Carolina, won't be long and I'll be there.

Come and Go Blues

Words and Music by Gregg Allman

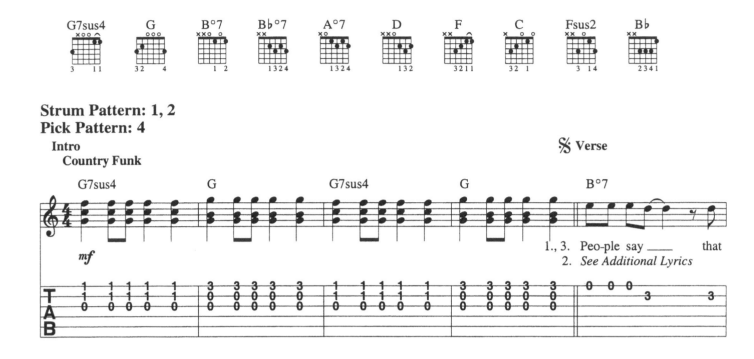

Strum Pattern: 1, 2
Pick Pattern: 4

Intro
Country Funk

%. Verse

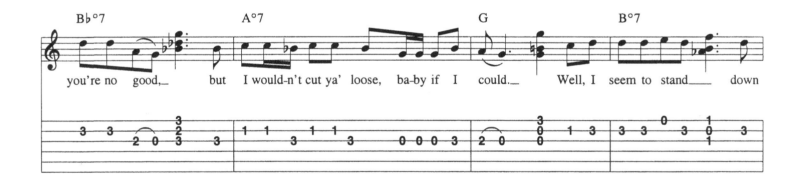

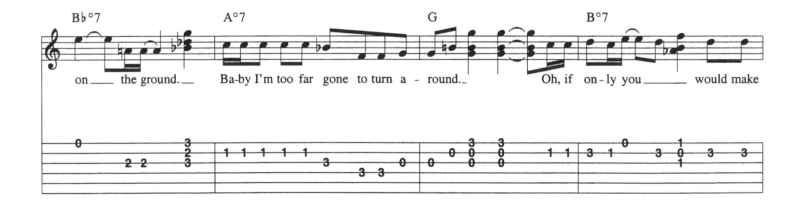

up your mind.____ take me where ya' go __ or leave me way be-hind._____ Lord ya' got _ those

come and go _____ blues. __ Lord ya' got _ those

To Coda 2 ⊕

come and go_____ blues. _____ Yes ya' do. Oh, and you got me feel-ing ____ like a fool. _____

3rd time, D.C. al Coda 1
play 3 times

Interlude

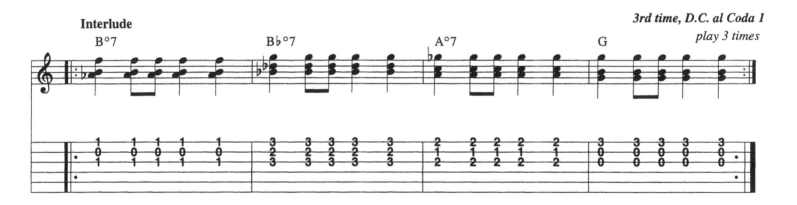

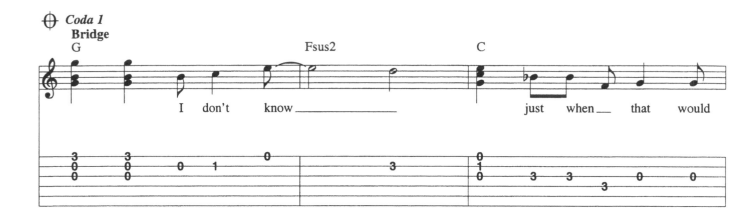

Coda 1
Bridge

I don't know _____ just when ___ that would

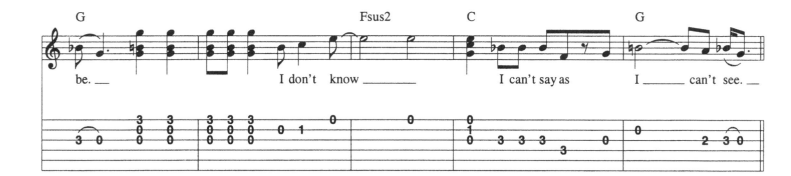

be. ___ I don't know _____ I can't say as I _____ can't see. ___

Interlude

Guitar Solo

play 4 times

D.S. al Coda 2

Coda 2

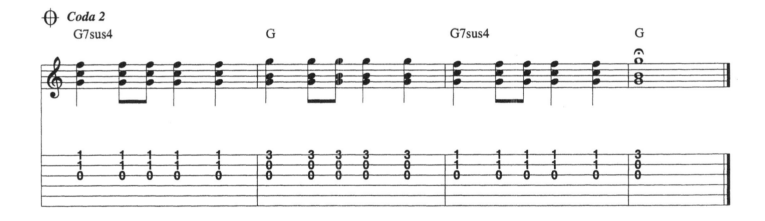

Additional Lyrics

2. Round and round and round it goes,
Don't ask me why I stay here,
I don't know.
Well, maybe I'm a fool to care.
Without your sweet love, baby,
I would be nowhere.
Here I stay locked in your web,
Till that day I might find somebody else.

End of the Line

Words and Music by Gregg Allman, Warren Haynes, Allen Woody and John Jaworowicz

bad, I had to fold _ my hands. _____ I al-most lost my soul. _

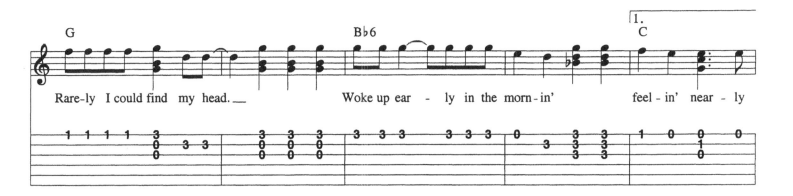

Rare-ly I could find my head. _ Woke up ear - ly in the morn-in' feel-in' near-ly

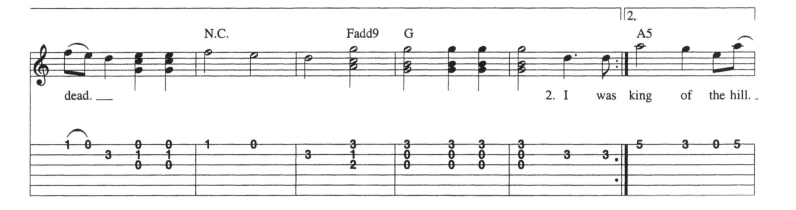

dead. _ 2. I was king of the hill. _

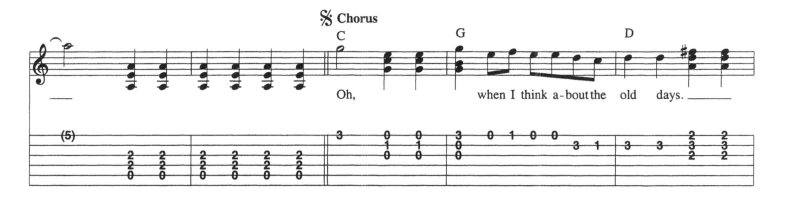

𝄋 Chorus

_ Oh, when I think a-bout the old days. _____

Lord, _____ it sends chills up and down my spine. ___ Yeah, __

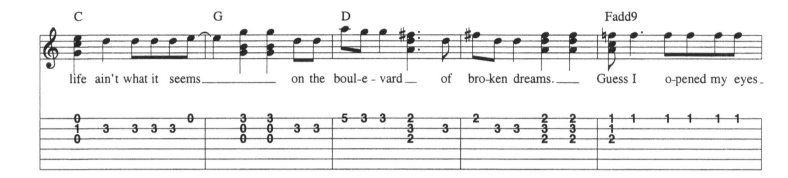

life ain't what it seems _____ on the boul-e-vard __ of bro-ken dreams. ___ Guess I o-pened my eyes __

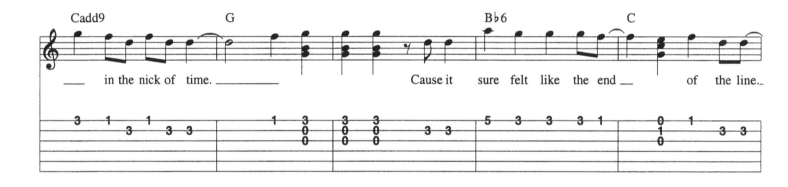

___ in the nick of time. _____ Cause it sure felt like the end __ of the line.__

To Coda ⊕

Verse

3. No mat-ter how hard I run, ___ I just can't get a-way. __

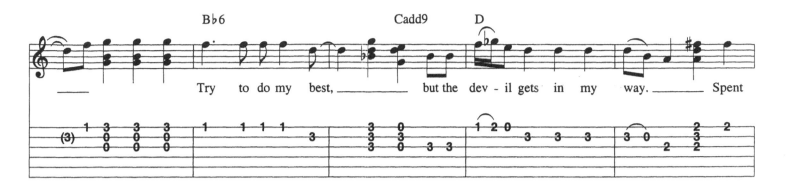

Try to do my best, _____ but the dev - il gets in my way. _____ Spent

most of my life - time down - town, _ sleep-in' be - hind ___ the wheel. Till it all - came

down _ to kill or be killed. _

D.S. al Coda

$\bigoplus$ *Coda*
D.C. and Fade
N.C.

Additional Lyrics

2. I was never afraid of danger.
   I took trouble on the chin.
   Mountains I have climbed,
   Could've killed a thousand men.
   I spent most of my life downtown,
   Sleepin' behind the wheel.
   I never needed anybody, I was king of the hill.

Good Clean Fun

Words and Music by Gregg Allman, Dickey Betts and Johnny Neel

Strum Pattern: 6
Pick Pattern: 3, 4

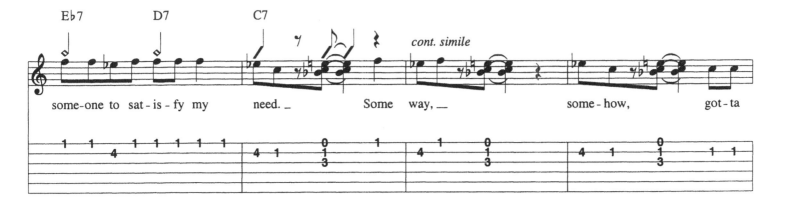

some-one to sat-is-fy my need. _ Some way, _ some-how, got-ta

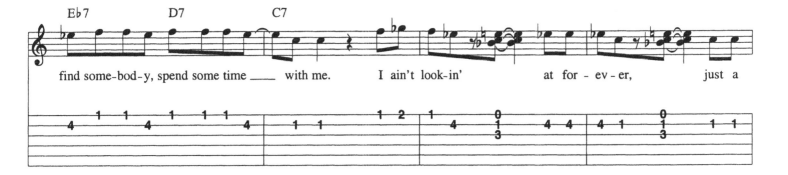

find some-bod-y, spend some time ____ with me. I ain't look-in' at for-ev-er, just a

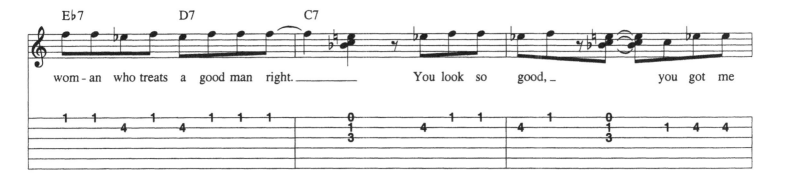

wom-an who treats a good man right._____ You look so good, _ you got me

think-in' you might sat-is-fy my soul all night. ____ There's no harm done. _ I

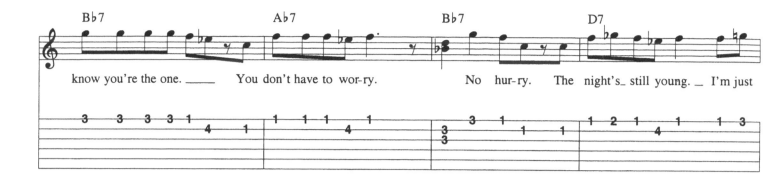

know you're the one. _____ You don't have to wor-ry. No hur-ry. The night's_ still young. _ I'm just

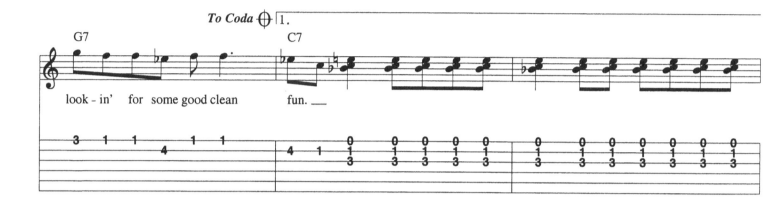

To Coda 1.

look-in' for some good clean fun. __

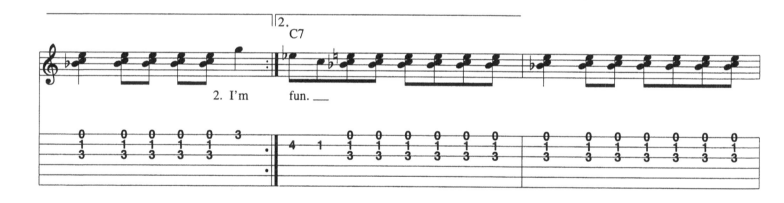

2.

2. I'm fun. __

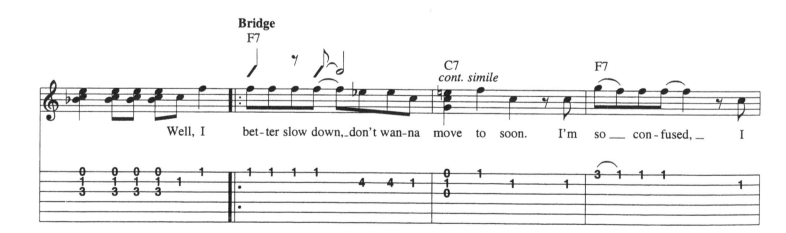

Bridge

Well, I bet-ter slow down,_don't wan-na move to soon. I'm so __ con-fused, __ I

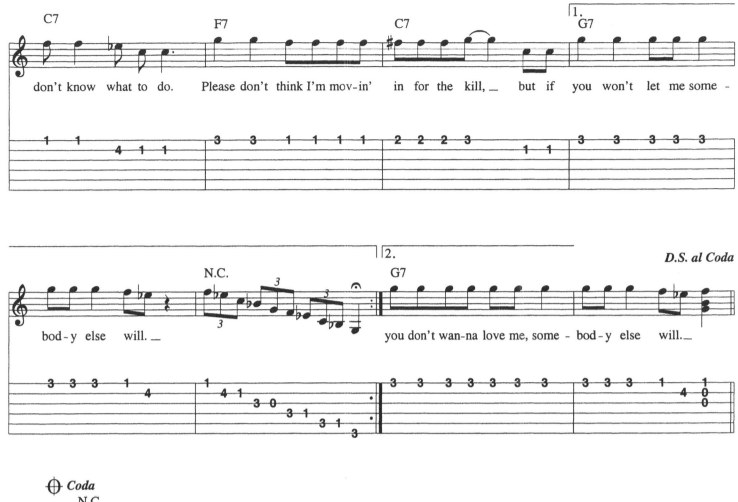

don't know what to do. Please don't think I'm mov-in' in for the kill, __ but if you won't let me some -

bod-y else will. __ you don't wan-na love me, some - bod-y else will. __

fun. __ Some good clean __ fun. __ Oh, __ ba -

- by. Look-in' for some good _____ clean fun. _____

Additional Lyrics

2. I'm lookin' for one woman who ain't always tryin' to put me down.
   I don't want nobody, givin' me that same old runaround.
   I ain't leapin', I'm just leanin', I'm lookin' for that good time thing.
   I can tell by the way you're actin', that you know exactly what I mean.

It's Not My Cross to Bear

Words and Music by Gregg Allman

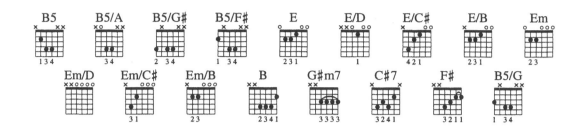

Strum Pattern: 8
Pick Pattern: 8

Intro
Slow Blues

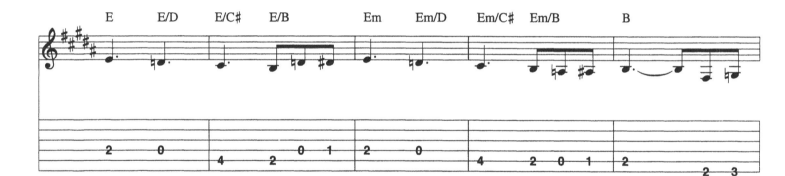

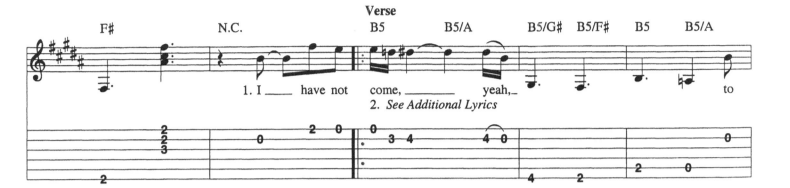

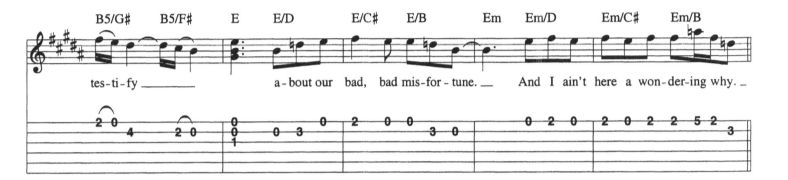

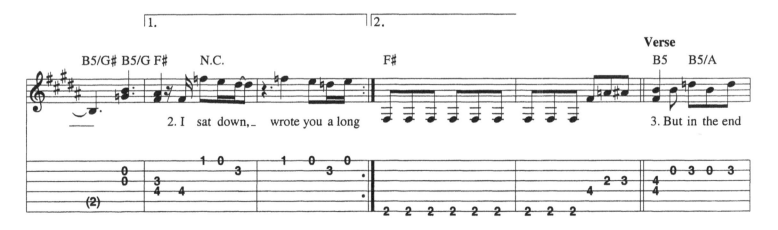

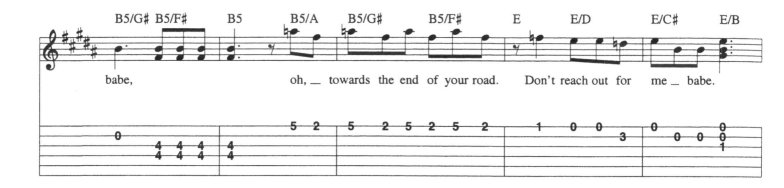

babe, oh, _ towards the end of your road. Don't reach out for me _ babe.

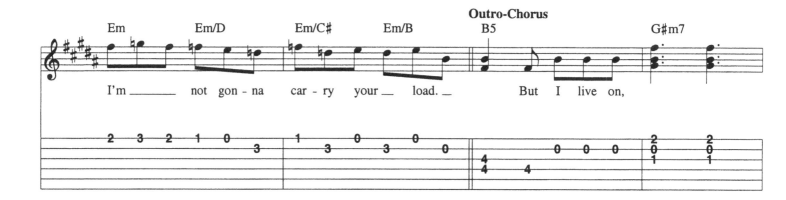

Outro-Chorus

I'm _____ not gon-na car-ry your _ load. _ But I live on,

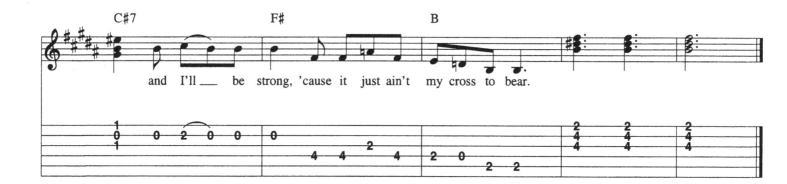

and I'll _ be strong, 'cause it just ain't my cross to bear.

Additional Lyrics

2. I sat down, wrote you a long letter,
   Was just the other day.
   I said sure as a sunrise, baby,
   Tomorrow I'll be up and on my way.

Melissa

Words and Music by Gregg Allman

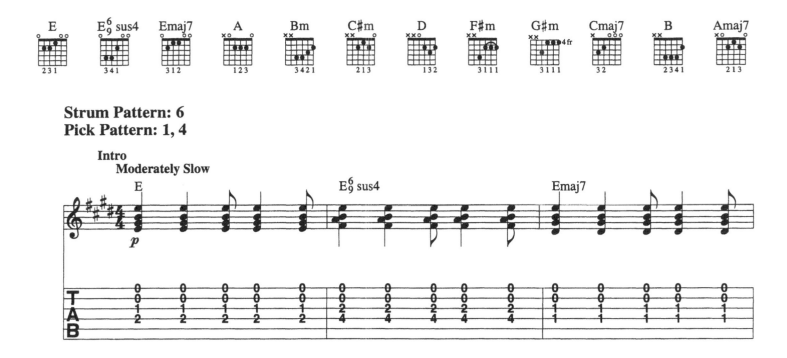

Strum Pattern: 6
Pick Pattern: 1, 4

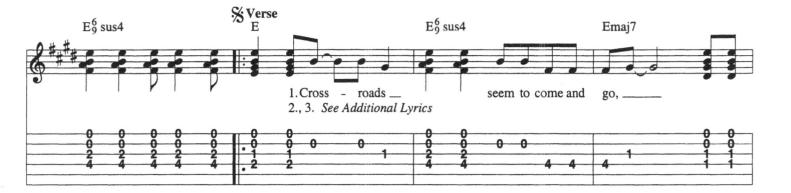

1. Cross - roads ___ seem to come and go, ___
2., 3. *See Additional Lyrics*

yeah. _____ The gyp-sy flies ___ from coast to coast, ___ know-in' man-y lov-in'

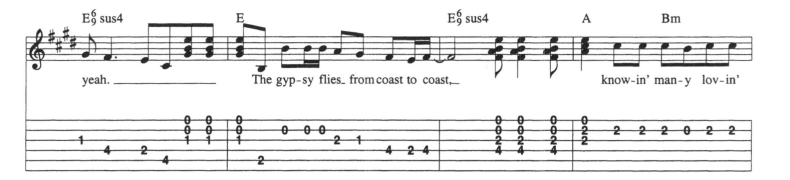

none, _____ bear-ing sor-row, hav-ing fun, ____ but back home you'll al-ways

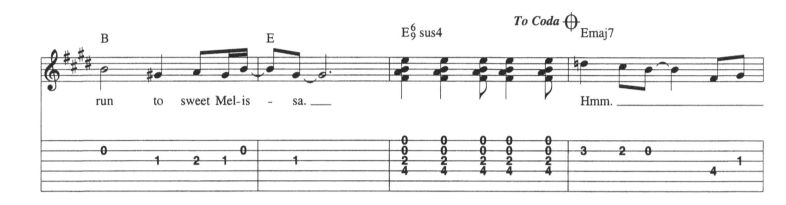

run to sweet Mel-is - sa. ____ Hmm. _____

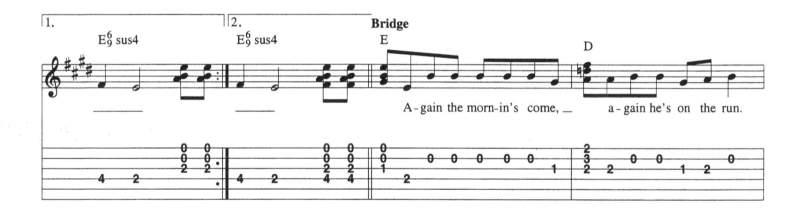

_____ _____ A-gain the morn-in's come, __ a-gain he's on the run.

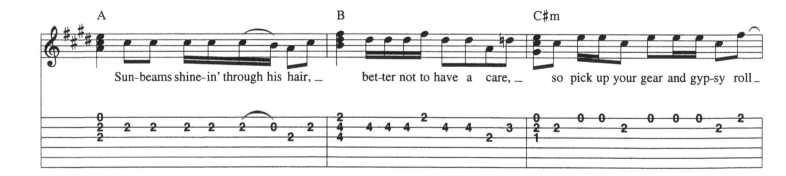

Sun-beams shine-in' through his hair, __ bet-ter not to have a care, __ so pick up your gear and gyp-sy roll __

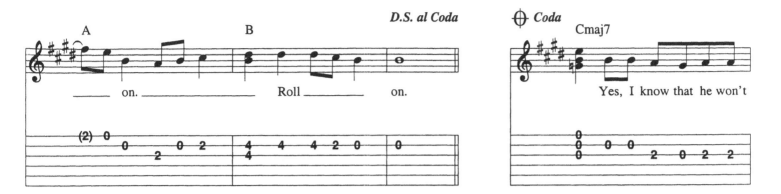

Additional Lyrics

2. Freight train, each car looks the same, all the same.
   And no one knows the gypsy's name, no one hears his lonely sigh.
   There are no blankets where he lies.
   Lord, in the deepest dreams the gypsy flies with sweet Melissa.

3. Crossroads, will you ever let him go?
   No, no, no, or will you hide the dead man's ghost?
   Lord, or will he lie beneath the plain?
   Or will his spirit fall away?
   But I know that he won't stay without Melissa.

Midnight Rider

Words and Music by Gregg Allman and Robert Kim Payne

Strum Pattern: 3, 6
Pick Pattern: 2

Additional Lyrics

2. And I don't own the clothes I'm wearin'.
   And the road goes on forever.
   And I've got one more silver dollar.

3. And I'm gone past the point of carin'.
   Some ol' bed I'll soon be sharin',
   And I've got one more silver dollar.

Pony Boy

Words and Music by Dickey Betts

1. Don't wor-ry ___ for me, well I'm al - right. ___
2., 3. See Additional Lyrics

Lord knows I'm hav-in' a nat-'ral good ___ time.

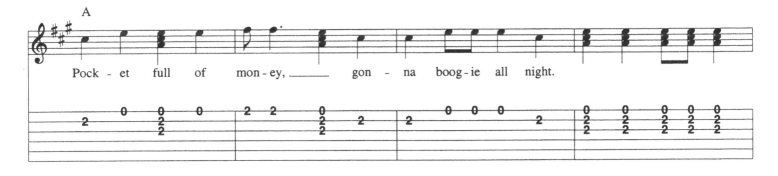

Pock - et full of mon - ey, _____ gon - na boog - ie all night.

Chorus

Ain't no - bod - y tell me that's a crime. When morn - in'

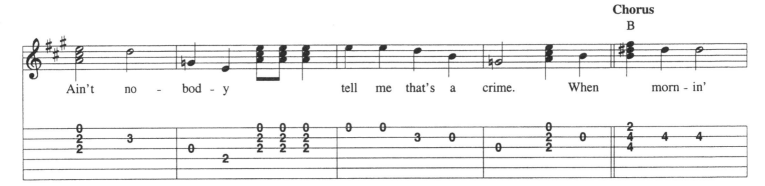

comes _ and its time to go, _____ Po - ny boy, _____ car - ry me home,

_____ al - right. Po - ny boy _____ car - ry me home.

To Coda

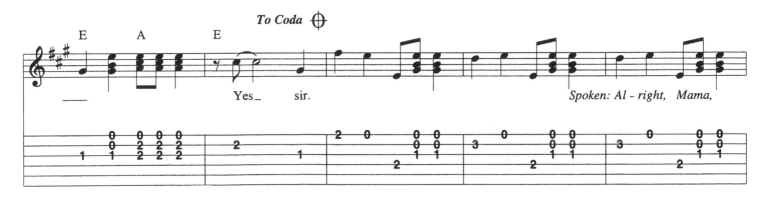

_____ Yes _ sir. *Spoken: Al - right, Mama,*

let me see you   do that thing now.

Interlude

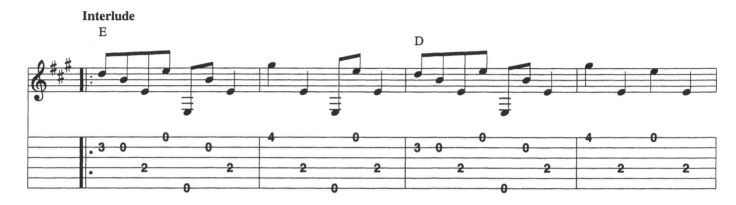

2nd time, D.S. al Coda

⊕ Coda
Outro

Additional Lyrics

2. Band is jumpin', and so am I.
I'm just groovin', can't stop movin'.
Lawman's got that old eagle eye,
Well, he's just waitin'. We're celebratin'!

3. Look out the door there, 'side that tree.
Well, that's my pony, he's lookin' after me.
Front feet doin' the shuffle, back feet, too.
Love them good old Georgia blues.

Ramblin' Man

Words and Music by Dickey Betts

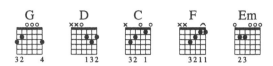

Strum Pattern: 6
Pick Pattern: 4

Intro
Fast Rock

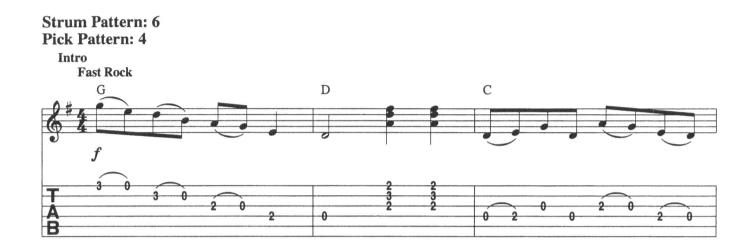

𝄋 **Chorus**

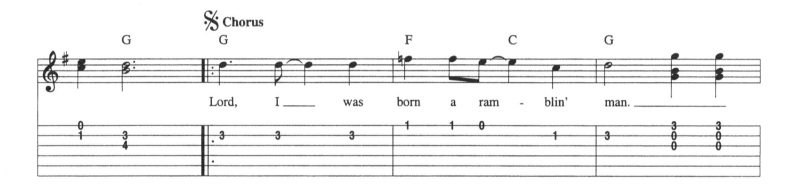

Lord, I ____ was born a ram - blin' man. ____

Try'n to make a liv - ing, and do - in' the best I ____

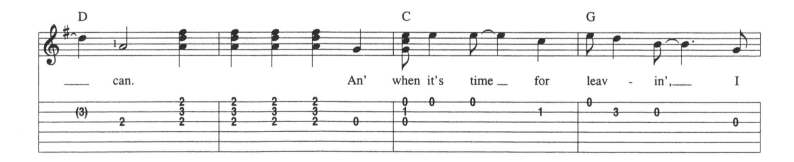

____ can. An' when it's time ____ for leav - in', ____ I

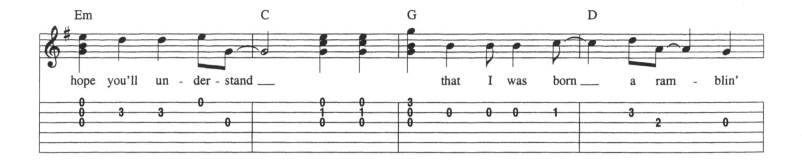

hope you'll un - der - stand ___ that I was born ___ a ram - blin'

To Coda ⊕ **Verse**

man. 1. Well, my fath - er was ___ a gam - bler down in
2. *See Additional Lyrics*

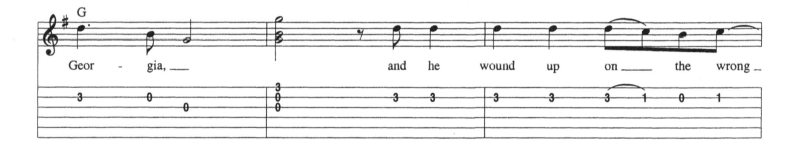

Geor - gia, ___ and he wound up on ___ the wrong ___

___ end of a gun. _____ And I was born ___ in the

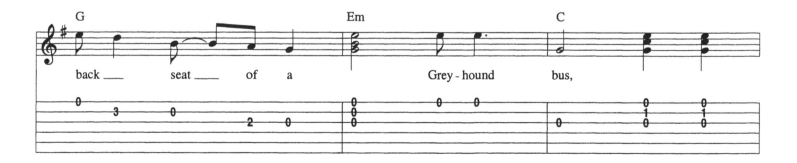

back ___ seat ___ of a Grey - hound bus,

roll - in' ___ down High - way For - ty One. _____

⊕ *Coda*

Outro

Lord, I ___ was born a ram - blin'

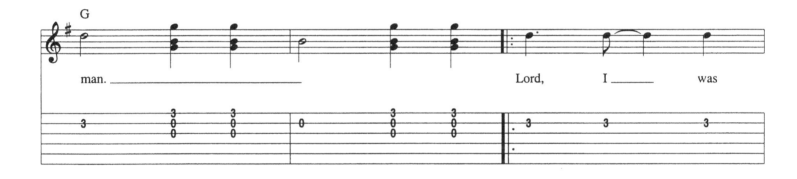

man. _____ Lord, I ___ was

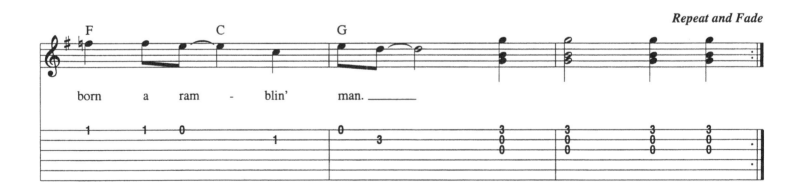

born a ram - blin' man. _____

Additional Lyrics

2. I'm on my way to New Orleans this mornin',
   And leavin' out of Nashville, Tennessee.
   They're always havin' a good time down on the bayou, Lord.
   Them delta women think the world of me.

Seven Turns

Words and Music by Dickey Betts

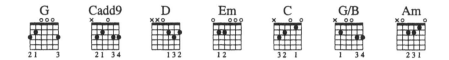

Strum Pattern: 3
Pick Pattern: 2

Intro
Moderate Country Rock

1. Sev - en turns _ on the high - way. _   Sev - en riv - ers to cross. _
2. *See Additional Lyrics*

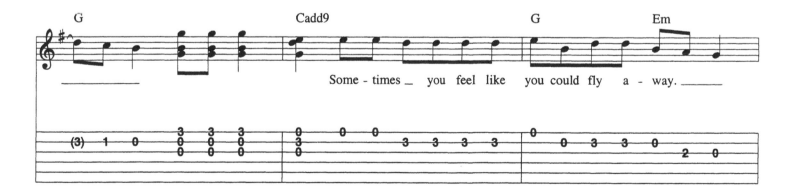

Some - times _ you feel like you could fly a - way. _____

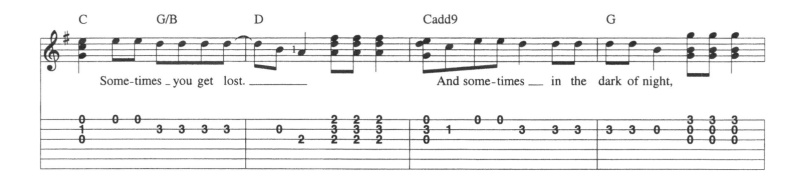

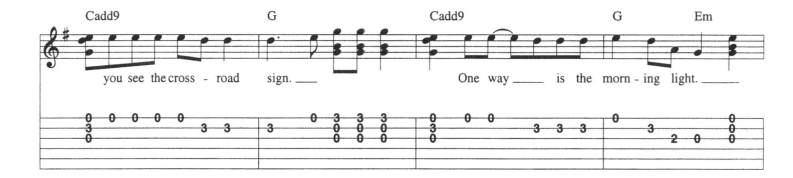

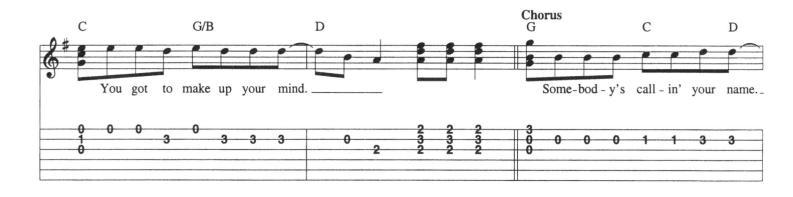

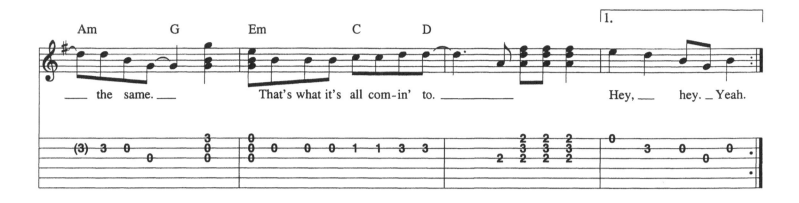

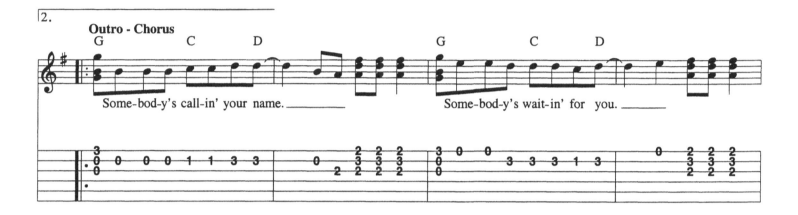

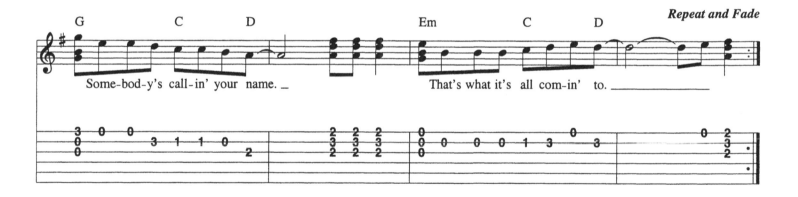

Additional Lyrics

2. Runnin' wild out on the road,
Just like a leaf on the wind.
How in the world could you ever know
We'd ever meet again?
Seven turns on the highway.
Seven rivers to cross.
Sometimes you feel like you could fly away.
Sometimes you get lost.

Southbound

Words and Music by Dickey Betts

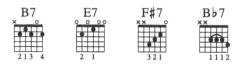

Strum Pattern: 1, 2
Pick Pattern: 2

1. Well, I'm south-bound, oh, I'm com-in' home to you. Lord, I'm
2., 3. *See Additional Lyrics*

south-bound ba - by, Lord, I'm com-in home to you. I got that old lone-some feel-in'

they some-times call the blues. Lord, I been Oh, you bet-ter be-lieve.

Bridge

Well, I'm south-bound.

Woo, hoo. ___ Aw, well, I'm south-bound babe.

To Coda ⊕

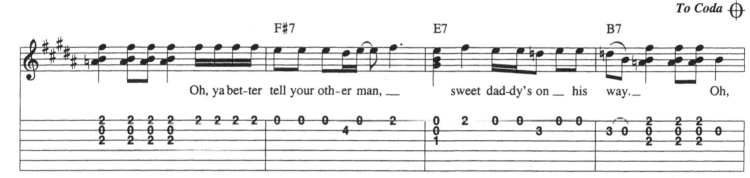

Oh, ya bet-ter tell your oth-er man, ___ sweet dad-dy's on ___ his way. ___ Oh,

D.S. al Coda
(take 2nd ending) ⊕ *Coda*

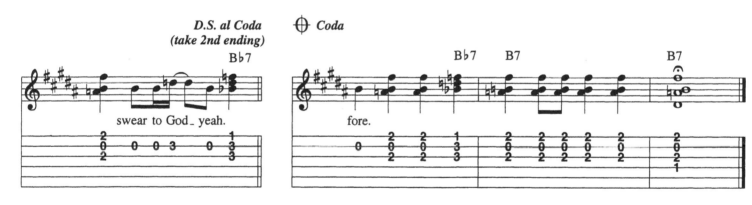

swear to God ___ yeah.   fore.

Additional Lyrics

2. Lord, I been workin' ev'ry night,
   Oh, travelin' ev'ryday.
   Lord, I been workin ev'ry night,
   Oh, travelin' ev'ryday.
   Oh, you can tell your other man,
   Sweet daddy's on the way.
   Oh, you better believe.

3. Got your hands full now baby,
   Oh, soon as I hit the door.
   Got your hands full now woman,
   Soon as I hit that door.
   Oh, I'm gonna make it all up to you.
   For all the things you should've had before.

Bridge Gonna go southbound.
   Oh, southbound babe.
   Ah, I'm goin' southbound. Yeah, babe.
   Make it all up to you,
   All the things you should've had before.

Stand Back

Words and Music by Gregg Allman and Berry Oakley

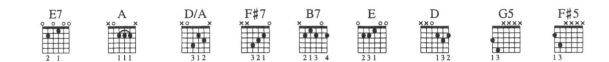

Strum Pattern: 2
Pick Pattern: 2

Intro
Swampy Funk

$ Verse

1. I re-call once up-on a time _____
2., 3. *See Additional Lyrics*

liv-in' was so eas-y 'n I felt so _____ fine. _____

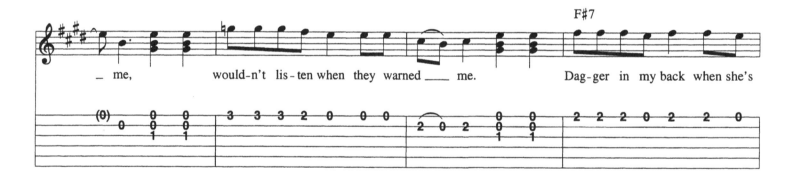

A   D/A   A   D/A A   D/A A   E7

My, my, _ my, _____   right be-fore my ver-y eyes _____   Sa-tan came with fire and burned _

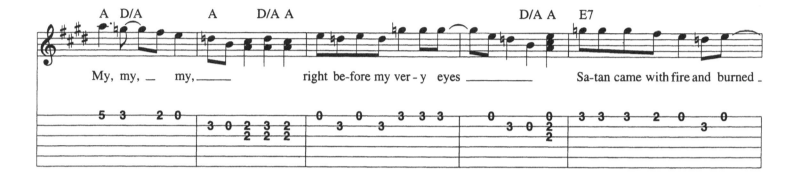

                                                    F#7

_ me,   would-n't lis-ten when they warned ___ me.   Dag-ger in my back when she's

        B7   E7

call-in' me hon-ey, would-n't stand back ___   for neith-er love nor _ mon-ey. _

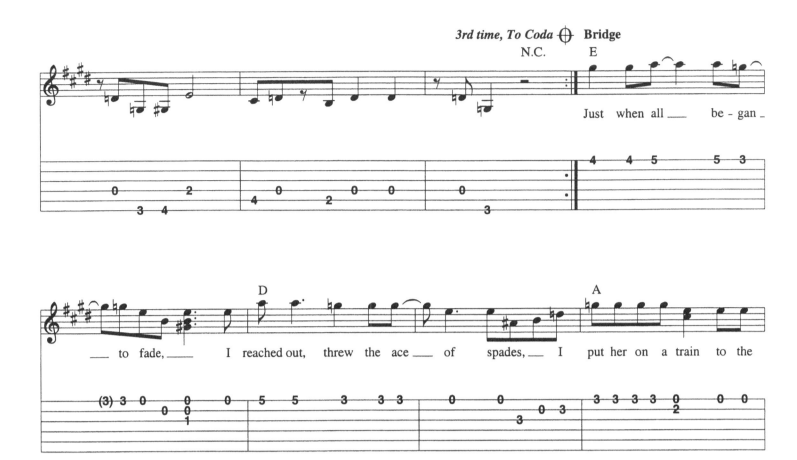

Additional Lyrics

2. Thirty minutes after my ship set sail
   She put up a sign and my house began to wail.
   And why, why, why, I couldn't see it in the little girl's eyes.
   She had such a way to fool me, Lord she had a way to fool me.
   And I would ask the woman,
   "Can you find it in yourself to please stand back,
   You ain't gonna move me."

3. Now that it's all over and gone
   Somehow I just don't feel so all alone.
   But lie, lie, lie, it seemed like such a waste of time.
   She did not ever seem to know me, now it's much too late to show me.
   But if I ever see that woman walkin' down the street,
   I'll just stand back, and try to move away slowly.
   Oh, yeah.

Statesboro Blues

Words and Music by Willy McTell

Strum Pattern: 1, 6
Pick Pattern: 2, 6

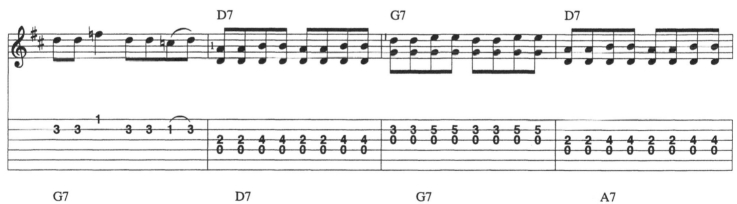

1. Wake up, ma-ma,

turn your lamp down low. _

Wake up, ma - ma, _

turn your lamp down low. _

Ya got no nerve _ ba-by,

ya turn Un - cle John from your door.

2. I woke up this morn - in' an'

I had them States-bo-ro blues. _   I woke up this morn-in' an'

I had them States-bo-ro blues. _   Well, I looked o-ver in the cor-ner, ba-by,

your grand-pa _ seem to have them, too.   Oh!

Interlude

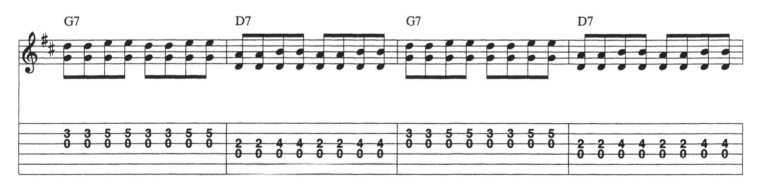

Verse

3. Well, my ma-ma died and left me, my pa-pa died and left me. I ain't good look-in', ba-by, want

some -one sweet and _ kind. ___ I'm go - in' to the coun - try, ba - by, do you wan - na go? _____

If you can't make it, ba - by, your sis - ter Lu - cille said she wan - na go.

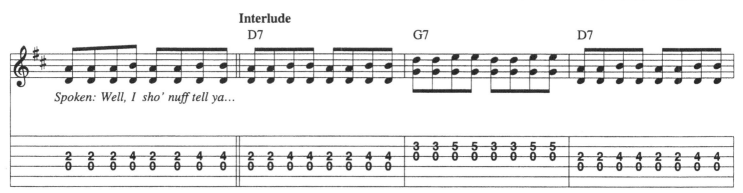

Interlude

Spoken: Well, I sho' nuff tell ya...

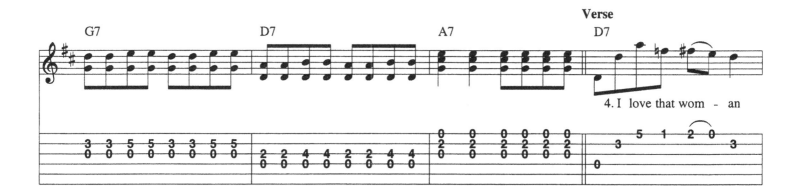

Verse

4. I love that wom - an

bet - ter 'n an - y wom - an I've ev - er seen. ___ Well, I _____ love that wom - an,

Straight from the Heart

Words and Music by Dickey Betts and Johnny Cobb

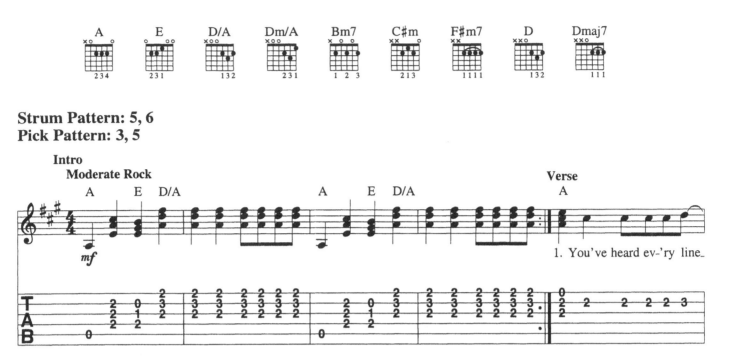

Strum Pattern: 5, 6
Pick Pattern: 3, 5

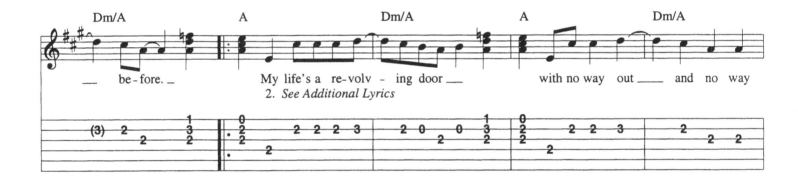

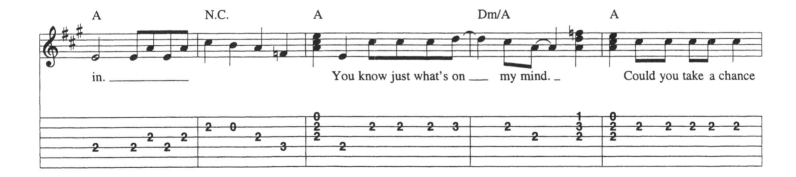

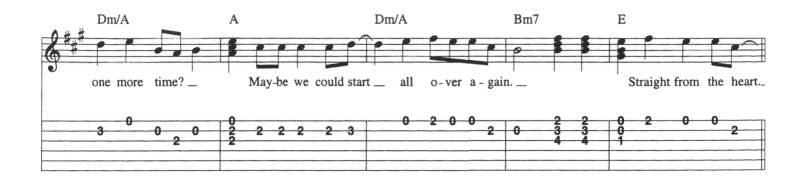

one more time? __ May-be we could start __ all o-ver a-gain. __ Straight from the heart.__

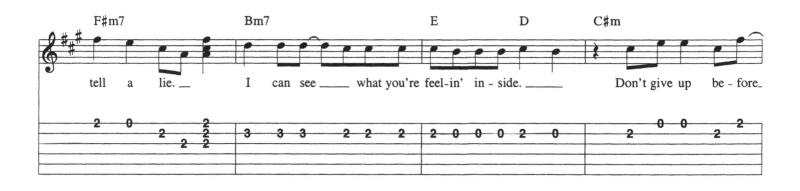

Chorus

__ Straight from __ the heart. __ { Ba - by my love. _____ }
{ Straight from the heart. _____ }

Your eyes __ can't

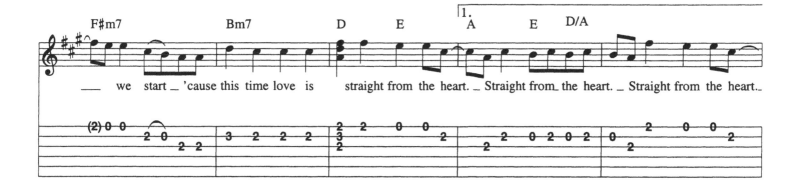

tell a lie. __ I can see _____ what you're feelin' in - side. _____ Don't give up be - fore__

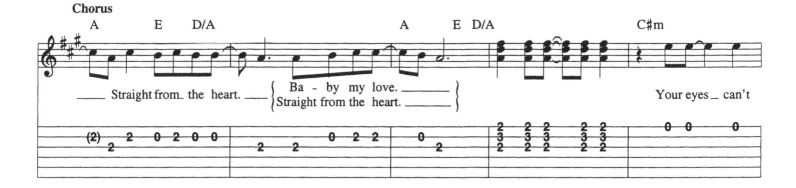

__ we start __ 'cause this time love is straight from the heart. __ Straight from__ the heart. __ Straight from the heart.__

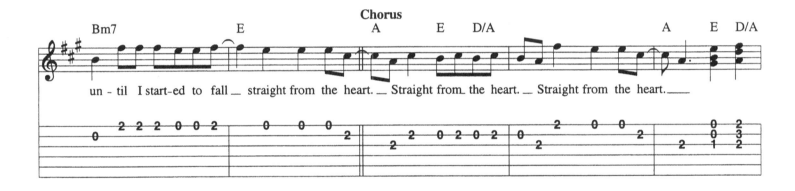

Additional Lyrics

2. I know that they're telling you.
I wish I could say that it's not true.
Love is so hard to find, but I never took the time.
I never let you in, please let me try again.

Wasted Words

Words and Music by Gregg Allman

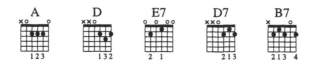

Strum Pattern: 6
Pick Pattern: 4, 6

Intro
Moderately

Verse

1. Can ya' tell __ me, tell me friend, __ just ex - act - ly __ where I've been? __
2., 3. *See Additional Lyrics*

Is that so _____ much to ask? __ I'll pay you back no mat - ter what the task. __

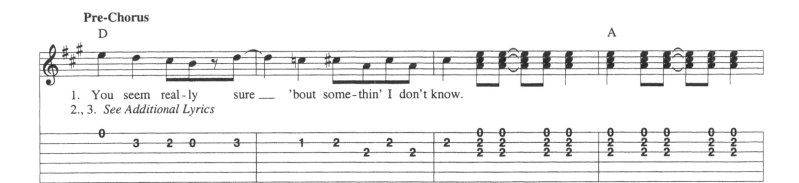

Pre-Chorus

1. You seem real-ly sure __ 'bout some-thin' I don't know.
2., 3. *See Additional Lyrics*

Take that load off, looks __ like you're just a-bout to go. __

Chorus

Wast-ed word's __ { al-read-y been heard, / so ab-surd. / will nev-er be heard. Are you real-ly God? Yes or / Are you real-ly / Go on home ba-by,

no? __ Sa-tan? Yes or

no? _____ Tell me now please, _ yeah.

Coda

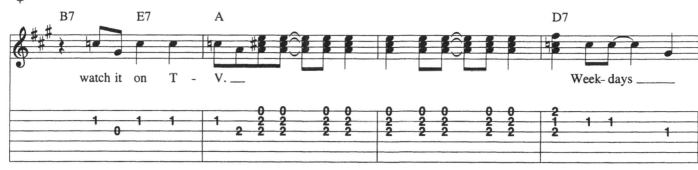

watch it on T - V. _ Week-days _____

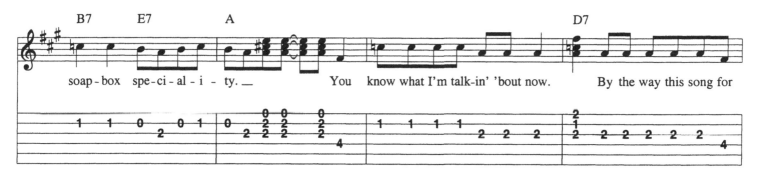

soap-box spe-ci-al-i-ty. _ You know what I'm talkin' 'bout now. By the way this song for

Outro

Repeat and Fade

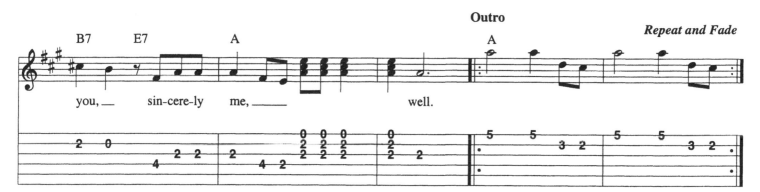

you, _ sin-cere-ly me, _____ well.

Additional Lyrics

2. Well, all day and half the night you're walkin' 'round, lookin' such a fright.
   God, is it me or is it you?
   I'll make a wager and I hope to lose.

Pre-Chorus 2. Time don't look like it about to fall, sure don't fall.
   Next time take the elevator, please don't call.

3. Well, I ain't no saint, sure as hell ain't no savior.
   Ev'ry other Christmas I would practice good behavior.
   That was then, this is now.
   Don't ask me to be Mister Clean, baby I don't know how.

Pre-Chorus 3. Ring my phone, now, ten more times and you will see.
   Find that broke down life and let it be.

Trouble No More

Written by McKinley Morganfield

A5   D5   E7#9

Strum Pattern: 3

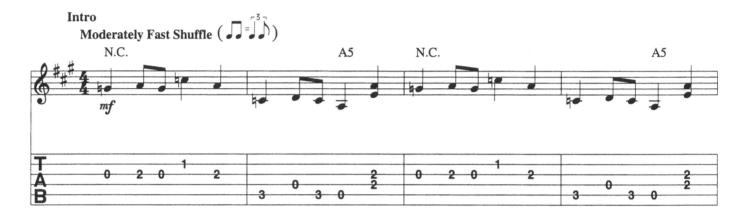

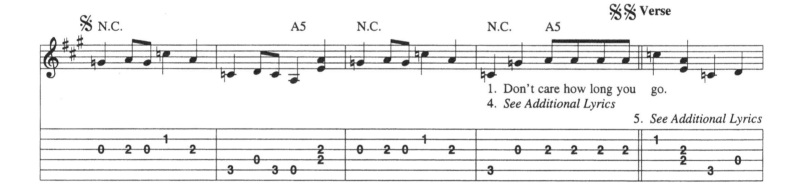

1. Don't care how long you   go.
4. *See Additional Lyrics*

5. *See Additional Lyrics*

I don't care how long you   stay. __   It's good, kind   treat - ment, __

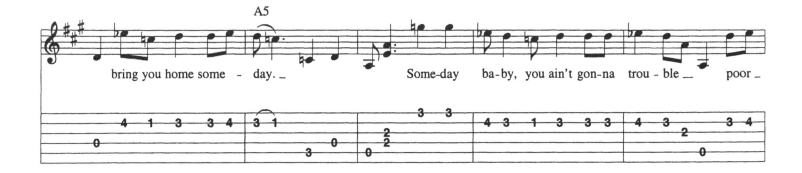

bring you home some - day. _ Some-day ba-by, you ain't gon-na trou-ble _ poor _

To Coda 1 ⊕
To Coda 2 ⊕

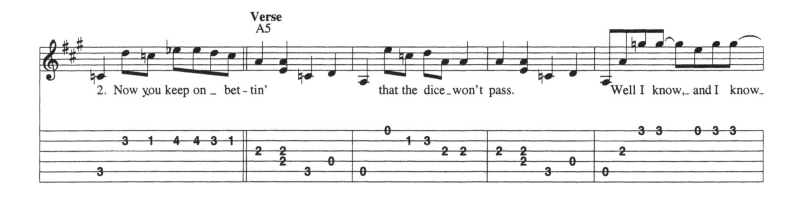

me _____ an - y more.

Verse

2. Now you keep on _ bet-tin' that the dice _ won't pass. Well I know, _ and I know _

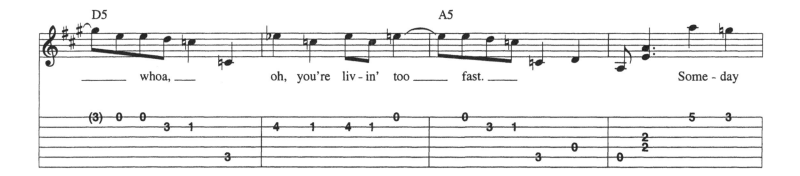

_____ whoa, ___ oh, you're liv - in' too _____ fast. _____ Some - day

ba - by, you ain't gon-na trou - ble _____ poor _____ me _____ an - y more.

Yeah. 3. I'll tell eve-ry-bod - y

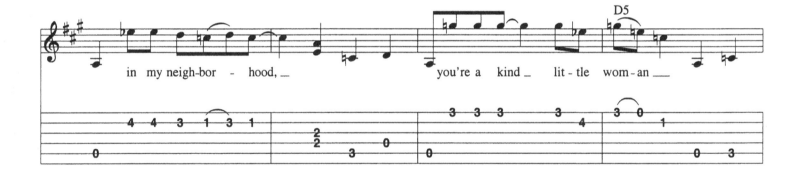

in my neigh-bor - hood, _____ you're a kind _____ lit - tle wom-an _____

but you don't _ do me no _____ good. _____ But some-day ba - by, _ you ain't gon-na trou - ble _ poor _

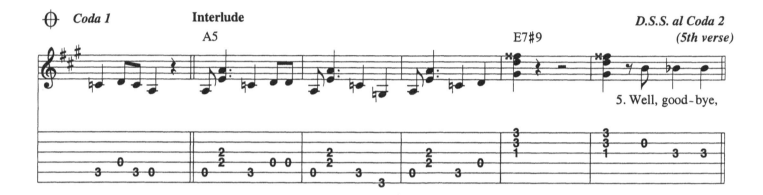

Additional Lyrics

4. I know you're leaving.
   If you call that's gone.
   Oh, without my lovin' yeah, oh, you can't stay long.
   But someday baby, you ain't gonna trouble poor me any more.
   Hell, yeah.

5. Well, goodbye, baby.
   Yeah, well take my hand.
   I don't want no woman no, who can't have no man.
   But someday baby, you ain't gonna trouble me any more.
   Trouble no more.

Whipping Post

Words and Music by Gregg Allman

Strum Pattern: 7, 8
Pick Pattern: 8

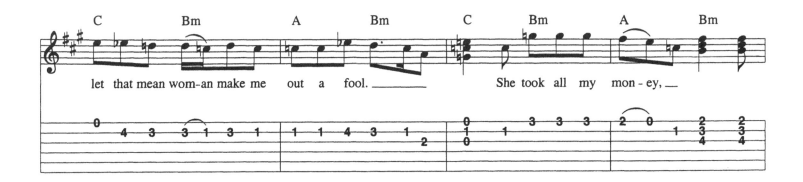

let that mean wom-an make me out a fool. _____ She took all my mon - ey, _____

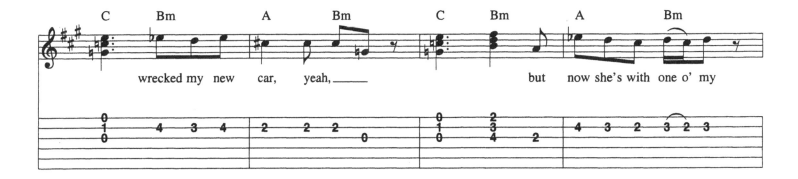

wrecked my new car, yeah, _____ but now she's with one o' my

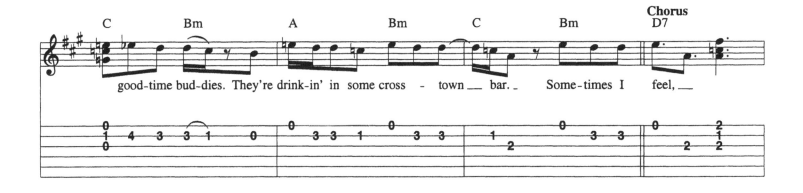

good-time bud-dies. They're drink-in' in some cross - town _ bar. _ Some-times I feel, _

whoa _ yeah, _ some-times _ I feel, _____ like I been tied _

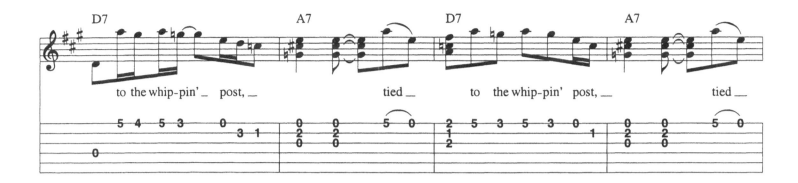

to the whip-pin'_ post, _ tied _ to the whip-pin' post, _ tied _

% **Outro**

to the whip-pin'_ post, _ an' Lord, I feel like I'm dy – in'.

D.S. and Fade
(take repeat)

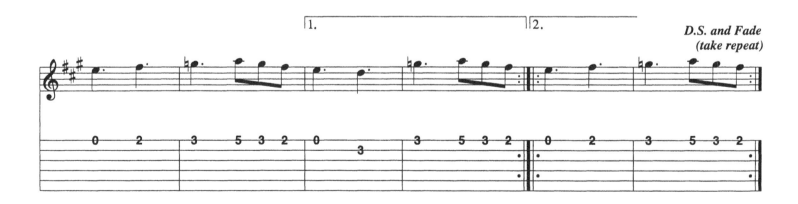

Additional Lyrics

2. My friends tell me that I've been such a fool.
An' I had to stand back 'n' take it baby, all for lovin' you.
I drown myself in sorrow as I look at what you've done.
But nothin' seems to change, the bad times stay the same an' I can't run.